RESUME WRITING

Stand Out in a Crowd with Your Enhanced Resume and Get Hired Instantly!

By JOANNE ROBINSON

Table of Contents

Introduction

Getting that dream job, the one where you know your experience makes you the best candidate means that you must be able to stand out in a crowd of several. Just take a look at your common job sites – ever notice how many resumes are submitted for one position? For highly desired employment, you could be looking at a volume of several hundred! The key to getting you through those interview doors and on your way to getting the position you deserve means enhancing your resume to catch the eye of the prospective employer. This book will focus on the strategies you need to create a resume that makes you stand out amongst the competition to help you get that job!

Your resume is essentially your story – one that provides the prospective employer with an overview of your work and educational history as well as your skills and abilities. The key to crafting a standout narrative is to create one that suits the needs of the individual who is on the other end assessing if you should be asked to come in for an interview. Control your story; create one that states that you are the best possible candidate for the position.

Research the opportunity and create a resume for the job. Use keywords that will hold the attention of the hiring manager. Apply strategy when selecting a resume format by choosing one that presents your experience and skills in the best possible way. Always submit an error-free document and make sure that proofreading is an ongoing task. Finally, submit a compelling cover letter that demonstrates your promise to the employment opportunity. With a bit of research and time, you can create a resume that allows you to stand out in the crowd!

Chapter 1: Resume Content

Create a Resume for the Job

This cannot be stated or stressed hard enough: the most important part of your resume is content, content, content! Your resume may be printed on the finest of papers. It may boast an elegant, elaborate design and it may be formatted to near perfection. All of this makes for a nicely presented package, but if your resume does not tell the prospective employer the story they want to hear; then it is just another pretty piece of paper that lacks substance. Your resume fails to stand out.

The fact is, your resume needs to be laser focused and strategically written to suit the needs of the job opening. In other words: you must create a resume specifically for the job to which you are applying.

The mistake most people make is taking a "one size fits all" approach to resume writing. Most people create the one resume and it's repeatedly used to apply for different positions. The issue with this is different job openings call for a varied skill set and a different set of work experiences. If you are using the same resume to try and land the Marketing Manager, Company ABC and the Administrative Assistant for 123 Corp., then between the two positions, it is highly likely you are missing out on the keywords and experiences needed to get your resume noticed by a recruiter.

The effective resume is a reflection of the job itself. What does this mean? Put simply, the resume that gets noticed is one that closely matches the skills and the experience the employment opening is asking for. A simple strategy for doing this is by taking the words used for a job opening and embedding them into your own resume. For example, Acme Corp is looking for a Social Media Manager.

The opening is as follows:

*"Acme's Social Media Manager will be responsible for **creating content** across all platforms. The position calls for a highly driven and strategic brand marketer who is able to **implement** Acme Corp's **content strategy** into relevant **blog posts** and **social campaigns**. Candidate must be well versed in **creating engagement** as well as **conversions strategies**. The Social Media Manager will be assessed by specific objectives including **Facebook likes**, **Twitter Re-Tweets** and **YouTube views**. This is a position with room to grow. Calls for a motivated worker who is able to **work independently**."*

If you are qualified for this position through either a mix of experience or education, you should be incorporating the very same words in your resume. In which case, your resume should look something like this:

- *Responsibilities included **creating content** for **Facebook, Twitter, and YouTube pages***
- ***Implementation** of company sales and marketing **strategy into relevant blog posts***
- *Developed successful **engagement strategy** that resulted in a 75% increase of Facebook post likes*
- *Increased Twitter page by 10,000 followers through innovative hashtag **conversion campaign***

This example displays what it means to create a story the employer wants to hear. In essence, the position is calling for a certain skill set and by using the job description in your resume, you are reinforcing that you are a strongest, if not the only, candidate for this opportunity.

Use Industry Key Words

Every industry has its "buzz" words. That is words that are used specific to a particular job industry. Making sure your resume includes these words helps to provide you with the edge needed to be able to make your resume stand out. In fact, it has become a necessity for a resume to include these words in order to make it to a place where it can be reviewed by human eyes.

The Internet has made it particularly easy for job seekers to submit a resume through a simple upload. With such ease of use, employers are finding the volume of resume submissions increasing at a rapid rate. The Human Resources departments of several large companies have turned to recruitment screening software to actually screen resumes. This means, you could be highly qualified for a position, but if your resume fails to include certain buzz words, your resume is weeded out and discarded; never to make it pass the software onto the desk and eyes, of someone who would be making the decision to bring you in for an interview.

Now, while these industry keywords are a must have for a stand-out resume, there is such a thing as "too much of a good thing" in regards to using them. Be careful to not overdo it; as using too many keywords turns into what is known as "keyword stuffing."   Instead, incorporate these keywords naturally into your resume.

Industry keywords vary. Take your time. Do the research. See what keywords apply to the industry you are going for and strategically use them in your resume. For instance, if I am submitting my resume for employment that falls into the customer service industry, I would need to use words such as, "relationship management" or "records management". If I were applying for a position in healthcare I'd use "clinical services" or "patient relations". The key is to research which words apply to your industry, selecting ones that speak to your experience and organically incorporating them in your resume.

Don't Forget Your Grammar!

 The absolute worst mistake you could ever make is using poor grammar or submitting a resume with even one spelling error. Now granted, mistakes do happen, and let's face it, most of us do not hold a degree in English, but the key to creating a perfect resume lies in making sure that you are using every resource to make sure that what you are submitting is beyond reproach, grammatically speaking of course.

There are several tools at your disposal to ensure that you are submitting an error-free resume. My favorite and to me, the most reliable, is technology. Using word processing programs such as Microsoft Word means that sentence structure and spelling is repeatedly checked. If that pesky fragment or an incorrectly spelled word does rear its ugly head, the error is highlighted and correcting the mistake is as simple as right-clicking and selecting the proper spelling, sentence structure or punctuation placement.

Having another person proof your resume is always a great idea. You know how it is, after spending a good 45 minutes going over that resume with a fine-toothed comb, the words begin to blend together. Sure, there is a space that shouldn't be there between the last letter of a word and a comma, but that gets a lot harder to catch when it is you proofing your own work. Having another set of eyes looking at your resume will help eliminate spelling or grammatical errors on your resume.

Chapter 2: Resume Format

Choosing an Effective Resume Format

Your resume tells the story about you: your experience and why you are the person who should be given the opportunity to come in for an interview. Depending on where you are in your work and educational experience, you need to choose a resume format that highlights your situation the best. Choosing the right resume will work towards enhancing your experience, skills, and education, whereas choosing a format that's not an ideal match may leave an employer with the impression that you are not qualified or even over qualified for the employment opportunity at hand.

There are three main resume format types that you can select from: chronological, functional and a combination. Which one is right for you? Well, let's take a closer look!

Chronological Resume

The chronological format is the most common form for resumes and the most widely accepted among prospective employers. This is also a format that is widely accepted by recruiters. Taking your most recent work experience and listing it first, then concluding with your oldest position, this format is the first type that comes into mind when a job seeker is looking to create a resume. For myself, on the resume editing side, about 85% of the resumes I look at are in the chronological format. Nevertheless, the chronological resume works best for a certain type of job seeker. If you are looking to stay in the same line of work or are looking for vertical movement within your current line of work, this is a format that will work well for your employment objectives. For instance, if I am a nurse submitting a resume for another nursing position at a different hospital, the chronological resume is the one that I would like to use to highlight how my past experience will be an asset to the current job opening.

Functional Resume

The functional resume template is the least used by job seekers and the least favored by recruiters, however, this format does serve its purpose. Allow me to provide a real life example to help illustrate the importance of this resume format. A few years back, I'd landed a position with a company making more money with more responsibility. Shortly after, I'd come to the realization that I wanted to do something I love – writing or editing. The only problem was, my work history comprised mostly of brand marketing experience. Nonetheless, I made the choice to throw caution to the wind and I submitted my resume for several editorial assistant, copy writing and proof reading employment opportunities. I did not receive a call back for an interview for any one of these. Can you guess why? You guessed it! While I was trying to change careers, I submitted a resume format that did not cater to my ultimate goal and tell the story of why I would be a good fit! Although I had a great amount of experience with writing and editing, my resume format did not reflect that.

The functional resume is ideal for career changers and those with gaps or difficult to explain patterns of employment. This type of resume does not focus on the occurrence of employment, but rather it focuses on the required skills and experience that you are able to bring to the employment opportunity. Again, while not the preferred, this format serves its purpose for a particular kind of job seeker. You should use this format if any of the above apply.

Combination Resume

Finally, the combination resume is one that is highly favored by recruiters. This resume format highlights your skills first – placing them front and center. The combination resume is exactly as it sounds: it is a combination of both the chronological and functional. The combination resume is formatted into two parts – one part highlights skills while the other part highlights your work experience. Again, many recruiters prefer this kind of resume as it allows them to immediately see if the candidate is qualified for the employment opportunity through a quick assessment of skills.

The combination resume is ideal for recent graduates, entry-level job seekers and those reentering the job market as more focus is placed on skills and abilities, not employment history.

Bonus Tip! When creating a combination resume, take a strategic approach to highlighting your skills. Be sure to list your strongest skills and abilities first! The skills you are not as proficient in should be placed at the bottom.

Chapter 3: Job Objective

To Include a Job Objective...or Not?

In the world of resume writing, there's been a continuing debate on whether or not to include an objective statement. There are those who feel that having an objective is absolutely necessary as it clearly defines to the prospective employer the kind of position or career opportunity being sought by those looking for employment. Others feel as if the objective is outdated and isn't necessary, the argument being that having an objective does not influence whether or not the job seeker is selected to interview and go further through the candidacy process.

There really isn't a correct answer. Choosing whether or not to include an objective statement is optional and is dependent on what your employment goals are. Take for instance the person seeking employment who is looking to land a specific, targeted position or role. An example of an objective statement such as: *"Objective: To secure a Senior Billing Clerk position within an established company."* This objective works well for a person seeking a specific position because it tells the recruiter exactly which opportunity within an organization is being sought after.

If you are looking to make a change in careers, a job objective becomes a must have. Without a job objective statement, one that makes clear that your employment goal is to change careers, the prospective employer is left to conclude that you want to continue in your current line of work. Going back to my own experience in trying to change careers, my resume was missing the objective statement. While I wanted to switch from a brand marketing role to a proofreading or editing position, the recruiter reading my resume wasn't aware of this and was probably wondering why I'd submitted my resume for an editorial assistant position when my resume had so much experience in marketing.

Again, choosing to include a job objective statement is up to the discretion of the job seeker. However, if the individual seeking employment is looking for a specific role or looking to change careers, the objective statement will help create a strong, targeted resume.

Creating a Strong Objective Statement

A well written objective statement sets the overall tone for the resume itself. A good objective statement is one that is clear, concise and targeted. You are given not more than a sentence to hold the attention of the prospective employer long enough for them to want to know more about your experiences. When done correctly, the objective statement will do just that.

Again, with resume writing you are telling a story the hiring manager wants to hear. An objective statement is a tool that can be used for this purpose. Your objective should focus on not what you want, but what you are able to contribute to the prospective employer. Your main goal is to make certain the statement is tailored to the job to which you are applying; therefore, you should highlight an overall ability that makes you the right person for the role. If you are effectively doing this – then your objective should be changing every time you submit your resume, as with different positions or companies, your story needs to change to match the job.

Your objective should state the talents you would bring to the position or company. Stay away from what I call typical resume language, the adjectives commonly used on resumes. For example, here are commonly used adjectives you'll find on a resume:

*"**Driven** sales person looking for an opportunity where I can utilize my skills in sales and marketing."*

*"**Accomplished** Brand Marketer..."*

*"**Experienced** and **hardworking** nurse seeking employment at a reputable healthcare facility."*

Can you able to imagine how many hiring managers see the same kinds of adjectives and verbs? The key here is to create an objective that specifically highlights the skills you are able to bring to the company. Ideally, your resume should be a refreshing change from the rest and not a carbon copy. I am going to take one of the three objective statements above and write a stronger one to illustrate how to create a more impactful job objective:

*"**Seasoned retail associate** with the **keen** ability to **surpass** sales goals by a margin of over 50%, looking for an opportunity where I can contribute to the **profitability of** Company X,Y,Z".*

In looking at the example above, "driven" is replaced by a more impactful adjective in "seasoned." "Salesperson" was too broad and not specific enough – that was replaced with a more targeted role in "retail associate." A specific skill was listed – the ability to meet and exceed sales goals. Finally, this statement finishes not with what the job seeker wants, but what they are offering to the company.

If used correctly, a good objective statement will hold the attention of the recruiter long enough to see that you are the perfect candidate to come in for the interview.

Bonus Tip! Use your job objective as an opportunity to use action verbs that will help you create a vibrant resume that stands out. So go ahead, crack open that thesaurus and get creative!

Chapter 4: Write a Work History to Impress!

The work history really is the "meat and potatoes" of the resume. Your past employment demonstrates to the hiring manager that you are not only familiar with duties and responsibilities of the job, but it also gives you a chance to show how well you did in your previous role. This is the part of your resume where you want to put your humility to the side. Now is the time to show off a bit of swagger – blow your own horn a bit. You want the person on the other end reading your resume to know that having you join their team would be every inch as beneficial for them as gaining employment is for you.

The work history section of your resume should be targeted to the position you are applying to (which ties back to the ideas expressed in Chapter 1 "Create a Resume for the Job"). The employment section you create for your resume should literally mirror your desired position.

This part of your resume must showcase both your achievements and results. It is not enough to simply state what your roles and responsibilities were, you need to specifically highlight how well you did your job. This is the mistake most job seekers often make when writing a resume; there is a rundown of responsibilities, but what's often lacking is what they were able to accomplish during their time in that position. The hiring manager reading your resume needs to know the potential you bring to the employment opportunity.

When drafting your employment history, always quantify or place a number on what you have achieved. For instance: "Effectively reduced company spending by 25%, saving $50,000 in costs." Use power verbs such as "executed," "controlled," "oversaw" and avoid typical ones such as "managed" or "handled".

💡 **Bonus Tip!** Take a few words used in the posting for the job opportunity and be sure to include these words in your own employment history.

Chapter 5: Education

Listing your education is another integral piece of creating your resume. The educational experience on a resume tells the hiring manager if the job seeker has the credentials needed for the posted employment opportunity. In addition to this, depending on your experience and the institution attended, listing your schooling may help to provide you with an edge over your competition.

Where your education is listed on the resume again depends on the type of job seeker. Recent graduates who are newly entering the job market, since work experience is relatively short, should highlight the educational piece. The educational experience should be placed before the work history. This section should include a GPA (if above a 3.0) as well as any academic honors and involvement in any clubs and extracurricular activities. Employment seekers with at least five years of work experience should place education after work experience.

If the job seeker does not have a degree then secondary education or GED may be included. If high school was attended but the individual seeking employment did not graduate, the resume should include dates of attendance.

Education should be listed by name of the institution, location, course of study and graduation or anticipated graduation date:

ACME College, New York, NY
B.A. English Literature and Composition, May 2015

Finally, any certifications or licenses received from a trade school may be included only if it applies to the job opportunity.

💡 **Bonus Tip!** List your highest level of education first.

Chapter 6: Make Your Skills & Abilities Shine!

Take your time. Do a little bit of research and include skills and abilities on your resume to make you shine out amongst the others! This section is particularly important because this is exactly what the hiring manager wants to see: does the person applying for this opportunity have the skill set needed to effectively perform in this role? The skills you include on your resume should be relevant to the employment opportunity you are pursuing. In fact, the abilities should be closely tailored to the job requirements and if done strategically, this will improve your chances of being selected to interview for the opening (this is where the research part comes in). For example, if the position you are seeking is in proofreading, listing skills such as "knowledge of AP style" and "Microsoft Word" would be an example of skills closely related to the job requirements.

Hard vs. Soft Skills

There are two different types of skills that should be used when creating this section of your resume. Hard skills are the quantifiable ones such as knowledge of a computer software or typing speed. Soft skills are ones that you aren't necessarily able to measure numerically. Examples of these kinds of skills include "communication skills,""time management," and the "ability to work independent of supervision." Be sure to include a good mix of both kinds of skills and again, they must tie into the open position.

Target Words

Target keywords are the skills desired by the prospective employer. Finding these keywords is as simple as reviewing the job description and finding the skills that are repeated throughout the employment posting. Once you identify these target words, and you indeed have that skill set, then you want to use these target words in listing your own skills and abilities.

♀ **Bonus Tip!** When creating your skills section, be sure to note what your proficiency level is with each one (beginner, intermediate, experienced).

Chapter 7: Personal Interests & Hobbies

Personal interests and hobbies may be listed on a resume only within certain parameters. Again, your resume is your story, one carefully written to illustrate how you would be an asset to a hiring institution. Therefore, everything that goes on your resume should highlight the abilities you would bring to the company. The same goes for your personal interests and hobbies. Only list those which would be an asset for you in gaining the position that you seek.

For instance, if you are pursuing a brand marketing employment opportunity in social media, then listing your Facebook Page with 50,000 followers would be an appropriate addition to your resume. For an editorial opportunity, including a blog on your resume would showcase your writing skills. If you do any volunteer work, then including this on your resume for an employment prospect in healthcare would work to enhance your resume.

If any of your personal interests or hobbies are relevant to the position to which you are applying and you are choosing to include these in your resume, this section should be included after the summary of your skills and abilities. This should be the final section of your resume.

Chapter 8: Listing References

To Include References...or Not?

When seeking employment, you will definitely need to have references handy for a hiring manager to check. Should those references be included on your resume? In general, references are not listed. There are a few sources that recommend listing references on a resume in only certain instances. As a resume writer myself, I would never advise an individual to list references for a couple of reasons. For privacy issues, you want to avoid including references. Also, your resume is prime real estate, you need as much space as you can to really build a compelling story. Listing references takes up valuable space that you can use with content to impress the prospective employer.

Most job seekers who create resumes make clear that references are available and ready to submit with the last sentence of the resume: "References available upon request." This, however, isn't necessary and should be left out of the resume as the availability of references is already implied.

Chapter 9: Resume Design

By now, you've got a resume with solid content. It has been scrutinized and updated to perfection. What's left now is putting it together into an attractive package that catches the eye of the recruiter. That being said, there is a careful balance that should be practiced when designing your resume, while an attractive resume can make you stand out – a busy resume – one that is too colorful or has too many decorative elements can be a turnoff to a recruiter.

DIY Design

There are two ways you can design a resume. If you have design experience, you can use a number of programs to create your own customized resume look. This method requires a good amount of time be set aside for formatting. You will want to determine a color scheme. The color scheme will be included in the header and borders. Select a hue that gives a nice burst of color to help your resume stand out. Be mindful of the color and make sure it isn't too bright or overpowering.

Pick a professional font. While the Comic Sans font is different and fun, it is not a professional font. The font may seem like the least important attribute of a resume, but it is actually quite significant. A bad font could potentially shift focus, taking the focus off your accomplishments. A font like

Times New Roman can get your resume lumped in with all the other unremarkable resumes. Some good fonts to consider are Garamond, Georgia, Arial, and Calibri. Be very careful to use the same to use the same font throughout the resume and avoid italicizing text.

You can also opt for visuals or images. A great way to do this is by inserting logos of companies you've worked for in the past. This works as an exceptional way of standing out especially if you have been employed by strong brands.

Resume Template

If you do not have the design experience, another available option would be to use a template. A major pro to using a template is the time-saving factor. By simply downloading a template, all you would need to do is add your content to preset tabs. A potential con is that templates do have a certain look; a look that recruiters are able to pick up on. Selecting an overused template will only work towards giving your resume a generic look. If you want to ensure that your resume stands out, a customized design would be your best alternative. Even if you do not have the design experience, finding someone with graphic experience to create one for you would be well worth it. You can have a customized layout created for you and treat it like a template. All you'd need to do is change content as you apply for different openings.

Bonus Tip! Minimize decorative elements. One example of such an element is the use of borders around your resume.

Chapter 10: Don't Forget Your Cover Letter!

Since your resume is the story you tell the prospective employer, the cover letter is the prelude to your masterpiece! The cover letter is an important piece to your resume since it provides the very first glimpse into your overall skills and the personality traits you would bring to the position in order to make it a success. This is an important summary of who you are and the potential you bring to the company.

Many employers make submitting a cover letter optional. In these instances, my recommendation is that you always submit a cover letter and I say this for a couple of reasons. First, taking your time to draft a compelling cover letter is a key way of displaying your commitment to the position. Secondly, submitting a resume without a cover letter depersonalizes your application. If you can submit a resume without a cover letter for one job opportunity, then chances are that you are doing the same for the next 20 or so openings. In which case there may be the perception that getting the particular job isn't that important to the seeker. I can't stress this often enough: always submit a cover letter with your resume.

Like its namesake, the cover letter really should read like, well, a letter to the recruiter. The salutation should be personal. The absolute worst thing you can do is write: "Dear Hiring Manager" or "To Human Resources Department." Be sure to address the recruiter or the individual who posted the employment opportunity by name.

The cover letter should be no more than one page. The content should include the position you are applying for and why you would like to be employed there. This is a chance to eagerly present yourself and make every effort to state what makes you a standout candidate for the opportunity. A cover letter is a great tool that gives the job seeker a voice amongst the other applicants; so be sure to maximize every opportunity to showcase who the real you is and why you would be such an asset to the hiring company.

Include information about the hiring firm's objectives and achievements; this displays to the recruiter that you have thoroughly researched the company as well as the position. Be sure to include your contact information and state when you are available to answer a potential phone call back from the recruiter.

💡 **Bonus Tip!** Leverage websites such as LinkedIn to gain better insight into who the hiring manager reading your cover letter is.

Conclusion

Your resume is your story; a marketing tool that is at your disposal to show the valuable asset you would be to the hiring firm. Creating a resume that stands out really isn't complicated; however it does take time and research to make sure that every section of your resume has an element to it that outshines your competition.

Take an approach that most do not when writing the resume: create a story the hiring manager wants to hear. Personalize the experience and speak directly to the prospective employer through target and industry keywords. Leverage your cover letter to display your commitment to the opportunity – make the recruiter feel as if this is the only opening you are willing to accept. Create a unique, eye-catching layout that immediately grabs the attention of the prospective employer. Proofread and edit until you are submitting a resume that is error-free. All these components will fluidly come together to give you the resume that will not only make you a stand-out, but outshine your competitor.